Birmingha
FRAME *by* FRAME

Welcome to Birmingham: Frame by Frame which tells in pictures the fascinating story of our city.

Birmingham today is vibrant, multi-cultural and proud. But a thousand years ago it would have been impossible to envisage that a handful of villagers and a couple of ploughs would one day become a city of a million inhabitants, a commercial hub and Britain's second city.

For hundreds of years it grew steadily, first as a busy but unremarkable market town with healthy industries in wool and leather, then as an area for metalworking with small forges springing up making nails, knives and bolts.

Then suddenly, with the Industrial Revolution, it exploded into life, becoming a city of innovation, craftsmanship and hard graft. It was a melting pot of ideas with the Lunar Society of Matthew Boulton and Erasmus Darwin, who drew in other great minds of the age.

Such was the pull of these men and their ideas that a 23-year-old named William Murdock walked from his home in Ayrshire to Birmingham in the hope of a job with steam engineer James Watt. His efforts were rewarded and Murdock, Watt and Boulton would become leading pioneers in the development of steam power that would drive industrialisation throughout Britain and the world.

Birmingham today continues to evolve and adapt. Although the city grew to prominence due to manufacturing and engineering, the economy is now dominated by the service sector and the city is one of the UK's largest financial centres outside of London.

Tourism, shopping and leisure industries are growing in importance with Birmingham now recognised internationally for its cultural, conference and exhibition venues.

Heritage Editor: Harri Aston
Written by: Sylvie Dalton
Designer: Ben Renshaw

Part of the Lost Britain Collection
© 2013 Trinity Mirror. All Rights Reserved

Managing Director: Ken Rogers
Senior Editor: Steve Hanrahan
Senior Art Editor: Rick Cooke
Editor: Paul Dove
Senior Marketing Executive: Claire Brown
Photosales: 0845 300 3021
Images: Mirrorpix, PA Photos
Printed by: William Gibbons

▶ **Total devastation** *The Bull Ring the morning after a heavy air raid, April 10, 1940*

Birmingham left battered by Blitz

A terrible cost of human life was paid by the bombing from the Germans in the Second World War, and the wounds inflicted saw that the city and its streets were transformed for ever

For most of us today it is impossible to truly appreciate the horrors of living through a war.

Highly-industrialised Birmingham was always going to be a major target for the German Luftwaffe bombing offensive and so it was. That the population managed to live with some sort of normality despite this constant threat says a lot about the human spirit and the madness that comes with war.

Cinemas, concerts and dances were still part of the daily routine as people attempted to live as normal a life as possible. Drinking tea from a flask while crouching in an Anderson shelter – which was little more than a piece of tin – knowing that any moment a bomb could wipe you and your family out was an experience which hopefully will not be repeated. To give some idea of the devastation, more than 12,000 houses were destroyed and 2,000 killed in air raids in the city.

During these tense years the responsibility to protect civilians was shouldered by the local Air Raid Precaution (A.R.P) services and Auxiliary Fire Service, whose reputations for bravery and efficiency became a cause for pride locally and nationally.

The Birmingham Blitz began in August 1940 and lasted until April 1943. In one two-day period more than 650 bombs fell on the city centre, destroying the Prince of Wales Theatre along with most of New Street and High Street. In total, it is estimated that in excess of 5,000 high explosive bombs were dropped during these years.

Photographs of the time captured unbelievable scenes of devastation. Familiar landmarks were bombed off the map, leaving a sense of disbelief, and families were wiped out, leaving friends and neighbours reeling in despair.

But there was also a sense of determination and great pride. The city's factories and workers were at the heart of the nation's war effort. Spitfires, Hurricanes, anti-tank guns and ammunition and thousands of other essentials were being rapidly produced. To thwart the Luftwaffe, factories were camouflaged to blend in with hills and surroundings.

Although evacuation of 25,000 Birmingham children had taken place early in the war to areas such as Leicestershire, Nottinghamshire and even as far as South Wales, many had returned when it seemed Hitler wouldn't attack.

Women were at the forefront of the war effort with nearly every able-bodied woman either joining the ambulance or other services or working on the land as part of the Women's Land Army.

Parks and school grounds were turned over to growing food. School children were even drafted in to harvest potato crops for local farmers. It seemed that every pair of able hands was willingly put to use in a concerted effort to beat Hitler.

▲ *Defiant attitude* Bomb damage at the Empire Theatre pictured in 1940

Getting ready Sandbags being piled up around the Town Hall in 1939

Royal visit King George VI visits Birmingham to survey the bomb damage in 1944

▲ **Clearing up** A team of soldiers pull down a bomb-damaged wall that posed a threat to public safety in 1940

▲ **Early preparations** Packing sandbags at the evacuation hospital in Birmingham in September 1939

▶ **Just the beginning** Petrol rationing in September 1939 as women from the Ministry of Supply vet applications for petrol coupons at the outbreak of the war

▲ **Striking back**
The anti-aircraft defences in Birmingham, May 10, 1941

▶ **Firemen at work** *Bomb damage to High Street in Birmingham after an air raid on the night of April 9, 1941*

◀ **Wreckage site** The original GPO bridge in November 1940

▼ **Complete carnage** Bomb damage to the Bull Ring, High Street, after an air raid on the night of April 9, 1941

Mass destruction Scene showing the destruction in Newton Street on the morning of April 10, 1941 after an air the previous evening

Emergency heroes *Firefighters attending the scene of destroyed buildings at the Bull Ring in the High Street, following the raids in April 1941*

▲ **Essential work** *A tank being assembled in Longbridge in about 1941*

◀ **No escape** *Birmingham City FC's St Andrews ground was hit during a bombing raid on January 21, 1942*

Just a shell Exterior view of Gresham Warehouse in Birmingham showing bomb damage caused by an air raid in April 1941

▲ **A city wrecked** An aerial view, captured on May 6, 1941, shows the bomb damage around St Martin's Church in the Bull Ring

▲ **The fightback begins** This image of tanks being built at the plant in Longbridge in 1941 shows the size of the effort made during the war

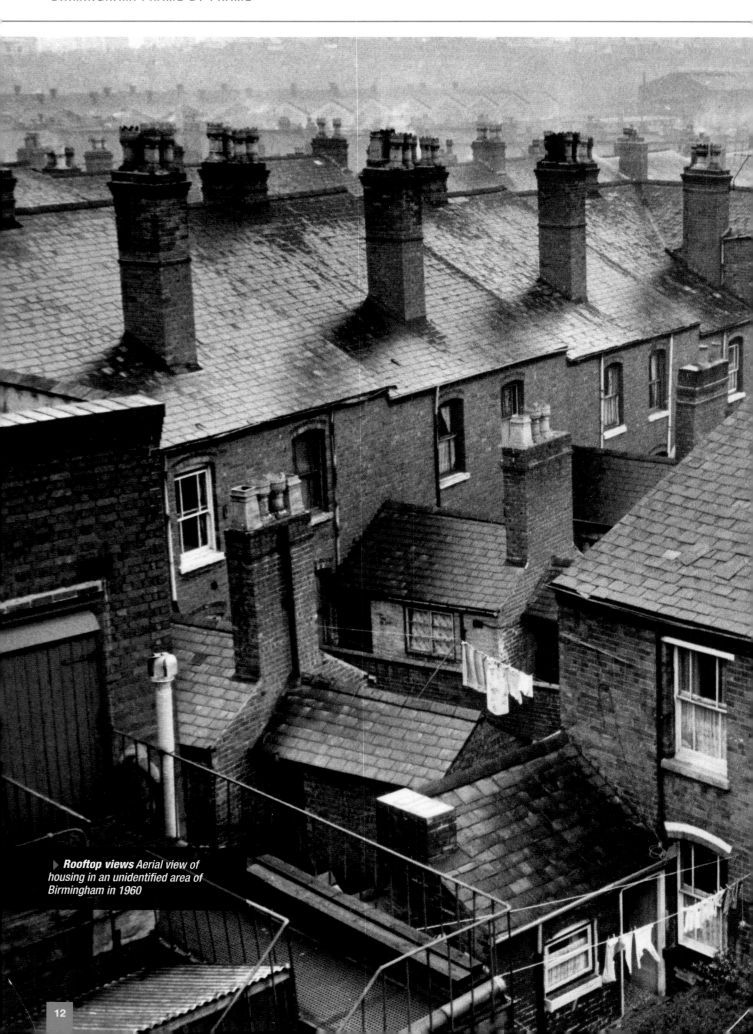

▶ **Rooftop views** Aerial view of
housing in an unidentified area of
Birmingham in 1960

Building on past for better homes

The explosion of population in Birmingham created a huge challenge to ensure its people were moved out of slums into proper homes

In the century leading up to 1901, the population of Birmingham increased from just over 70,000 to 500,000.

Birmingham was one of the fastest growing cities in the country, attracting not only workers from the surrounding villages but from Wales and Ireland, and even welcoming skilled artisans from the continent.

With such an influx, there was always going to be pressure on housing. The need to build was immense and with the centre of the city becoming increasingly industrialised, the heaviest burden fell here with the larger Georgian houses being replaced with dense developments for the working-class and poor.

These were inferior built back-to-back homes, usually two up, two down without toilets or washing facilities and with poor ventilation. A stand-pipe for fresh water and a toilet would be provided in a courtyard and shared by several households. Often, water was only available from the stand-pipe for short periods during the week, with residents forced to use wells contaminated with sewage the rest of the time.

The toilets were completely inadequate and flowed onto the streets. Bootless and ragged children often played in squalid conditions. It was no surprise that disease was rife.

Any green spaces in the city centre were quickly being eaten up. Those who could afford to move out did so. The introduction of trains and trams helped make this possible with the suburbs becoming popular as builders offered better quality housing for the middle-class and artisan worker. Meanwhile, the hastily thrown up housing in the centre of Birmingham disintegrated into slums. Life was grim for many living in Hockley, Lozells, Nechells, Duddeston, Saltley, Deritend, Highgate and Ladywood. Only Edgbaston seemed to escape the ravages of poverty.

But the centre of Birmingham was rapidly evolving and, by the 1850s, with the building of first New Street Station, then Snow Hill, a large number of slums were already being cleared.

The problems were not going unnoticed amongst the city's political elite, and in the 1870s, various changes were put into place. The city's mayor, Joseph Chamberlain, forcibly purchased Birmingham's waterworks, creating the Birmingham Corporation Water Department with the expressed desire to see improved access to water for the public.

And five years later he spearheaded plans for slum clearance by proposing the building of Corporation Street, with the slum dwellers eventually being rehoused in the suburbs.

Despite these efforts many of the city's industrial workers still lived in poor conditions and slums would remain well past the 1950s. It was not until the 1970s that the slum clearance was finally completed.

Many sites were replaced with council estates and tower blocks. These were initially hailed as the answer to new healthy and modern housing but would themselves, over time, fall into a state of disrepair to become sink estates.

▲ **Shocking poverty** *Children play amongst the wreckage of abandoned cars, old iron and decayed vegetable matter which have been dumped on cleared redevelopment sites in Knutsford Street, Balsall Heath, in November 1967*

Squalor
A burnt-out car in the alleyway behind derelict houses in May 1966

Deprivation
Children playing outdoors in the 1970s

▲ **Slum living** The kitchen of a slum home in August 1959

▲ **Cramped conditions**
Shirley Jones is pictured in the kitchen of her home in Aston with two young children on September 11, 1969

▶ **Community spirit** Residents of Allison Street outside their properties

▶ **Grim reality** *Rita Williams and her five-year-old son, John, pictured outside the front of their house in Wenman Street, Balsall Heath, on May 20, 1973*

▲ **Poverty** *A family outside their home in Birmingham in the early 20th century*

▶ **Resident's fury** *The rubbish-strewn scene behind Patricia Bambury's wool shop on Edward Road, Balsall Heath, in 1973*

Empty land *Ladywood slums in July 1954*

Local character *Alice Swanton sits in her decaying terrace house in George Place, Ladywood, accompanied by stray cats of the area in April 1968*

▲ *Boarded buildings*
Edward Street in Ladywood in April 1967

▶ *Area devastation*
Slum housing in Ladywood, pictured in July 1954

Dereliction all around Children play and collect firewood amongst the wreckage of houses awaiting demolition in Balsall Heath in December 1970

Dangerous location Slum housing near the city centre in Birmingham. Children playing outside beside a knocked-down wall in March 1969

Unsanitary homes Back-to-back houses in Aston in 1940

Another day Workers stream out of the Longbridge motor plant in Birmingham after the end of their shift on October 2, 1966

Heart of industry and employment

Birmingham was home to a host of giants of manufacturing and helped drive the country to unprecedented economic prosperity in the years following the Second World War

▲ *Factory labour* *Women workers armature winding at the Lucas building at Great King Street, Birmingham, photographed in the early 1920s*

The City of a Thousand Trades it has been known for generations but the decades after the Second World War saw a boom-time in Birmingham that not only drove the city but also the country to an age of unprecedented economic prosperity. Birmingham had become a shining beacon of all that was possible.

Jobs were plentiful, spirits soared and the buzz of the city was electrifying, literally, as the manufacturing of electrical equipment and motor vehicles led Britain out of the darkness of the war years.

The city was home to a host of world-leading giants of manufacturing including Dunlop Tyres, Cadbury, Land Rover, Jaguar, Lucas and HP Sauces to name but a few. And of course, the biggest of all – Austin Motors, later to become British Leyland and eventually Rover.

These were big hitters; Dunlop alone could at one time lay claim to owning the biggest factory on the planet and by the mid-1950s employed in excess of 10,000 workers.

The imposing Fort Dunlop might dominate the skyline in Erdington but there were plenty more industries making their mark in the city and surrounding areas.

By the 1950s, Jaguar, having out grown the Coventry site, expanded to Birmingham and the ever-popular cars are still assembled today at Castle Bromwich under the Jaguar Land Rover banner.

Car manufacturing also led to a growth of car component industries and few can outshine the spirit of enterprise displayed by Hockley's Joseph Lucas. Joseph eked out an existence selling paraffin from a cart to support his six children.

From these humble beginnings in the 19th century grew the hugely successful Lucas Industries – a leading manufacturer of components for the motor and aerospace industries.

Although car manufacturing and associated industries have dominated the West Midlands, confectionery and food manufacturers have also produced world-class brands.

HP sauce, with its distinctive label, was given its name early on after rumours circulated that the sauce was being served in the restaurant at the Houses of Parliament.

Nottingham grocer Frederick Gibson Garton first came up with the recipe – and the name – but sold it to Edwin Samson Moore for £150 to settle some bills. Samson Moore, founder of the Midlands Vinegar Company – which would later become HP Foods – then launched HP Sauce in 1903. For many years this sauce was produced at the Tower Road factory site in Aston, with its famous overhead pipe carrying vinegar from one side of the plant across the A38 to the other.

No chapter on industry would be complete without Cadbury. And it all started in Bull Street with Quaker John Cadbury selling tea, coffee and his own drinking chocolate.

Thirty years later, The Cadbury Brothers of Birmingham were manufacturers of chocolate and cocoa to Queen Victoria. John's sons continued their father's success and soon an assortment of chocolate-covered products were being produced. New premises were sought which would provide good transport links by canal and rail and Bournbrook Estate was bought, developed and renamed Bournville to reflect the fashion for French chocolate at this time.

Chocolate checking Women working on a production line at Cadbury's, checking the chocolates, on April 27, 1966

◀ **Sweet job** Women coating chocolates at Cadbury's Bournville works, October 28, 1932

▶ **Eggs up** Lyn Hamblin takes trays of half Easter eggs off the conveyor, ready for filling and wrapping, at Cadbury on January 4, 1984

◀ **Special visitor** Senator Edward Kennedy chats to Cadbury workers in Bournville as part of a five-day tour of the UK on September 13, 1971

▶ **Loyal worker** Dave Hopkins at work on June 19, 1985 in the panel shop. He had worked at Jenson Motors for 40 years

▶ **Fine art** Silversmith Harry Brown makes a hinge for a bracelet at his Birmingham workshop in January 1970

▶ **Sales success** Sir George Farmer congratulating production manager James Lawrence as the 750,000th Land Rover came off the assembly line on July 1, 1971

▲ **Don't drop it!** On October 27, 1978, the largest tyre that had ever been made to date arrived at Fort Dunlop's test centre in Birmingham. It weighed two-and-a-quarter tonnes and was pictured above a Mini 1275 GT, which used Dunlop's smallest road tyre

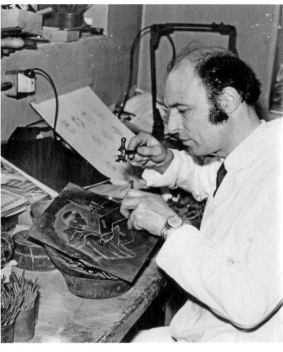

▲ **Gilding the bronze** Philip Moody, 39, at work in Birmingham's Jewellery Quarter in December 1969. Working on a bronze trademark for a firm of leather embossers and gilders, he has knocked up the 'masses' of the design from the reverse side and has now turned the sheet of bronze to trace the outlines

Warm welcome Margaret Thatcher, then the leader of the Opposition, receives a kiss from a Birmingham butcher in 1977

▲ **Famous name**
The Rover site at Hay Hall Road, Tyseley, April 29, 1976

▶ **Preparation work** *Workmen adding the finishing touches to the new trim and assembly hall at Longbridge for British Leyland's new Mini Metro on May 4, 1979*

▲ **Car classic** Men at work in the West Bromwich factory where Jensen Interceptor and FF cars were being produced on April 3, 1970

▶ **Working the line** In a quiet and deserted East Works at Longbridge, car engines are covered with brown paper while a maintenance squad overhauls the track on July 29, 1969

◀ **Industrious area** Men at work in the Jensen Motors' car factory, working on the Austin-Healey in 1966

▶ **On song** Pupils gathered for assembly at King Edwards School, Five Ways, Birmingham, on March 28, 1958

Learning the old fashioned way

Schools have changed a great deal over the decades but, for many of us, they remain the places where we spent some of the best days of our lives

▲ Hard at work
Classroom scene at St Nicholas Catholic Primary School, Sutton Coldfield, in September 1968

Life for most children was incredibly tough before, during and even after the industrial revolution – that's if they survived at all.

For centuries, education was generally the preserve of the nobility or wealthy. As early as the 1550s, Birmingham could boast its own "free" grammar school in New Street, created by Royal Charter by King Edward VI. The foundation still exists today and its schools are well known in the city.

There was little formal education and no state provision but in the mid-18th century the Sunday School movement tentatively began, initiated by Robert Raikes, proprietor of the Gloucester Journal. One of its first targets were boys from the slums.

Sunday was selected as the boys were often working in the factories the other six days – these were children with an average age of 10, working in excess of a 12-hour day. Sunday Schools offered an opportunity to better themselves and they grabbed it.

From these, Sunday Schools grew the concept of church schools.

By 1851 the Church of England had established 17,000 elementary schools. The idea was to create a church school in every parish to provide a Christian education for the poor but those who could were obliged to pay the "school pence". Other denominations were also building schools.

By the late 1860s the city had become a hotbed of educational campaigning. Joseph Chamberlain favoured free, secular, compulsory education and he was joined by other city politicians in forming the Birmingham Education League which would eventually become the influential National Education League.

In 1870, school boards were given powers to open industrial schools.

The industrial school was designed to provide for boys aged 7-14 who were not yet criminals but were thought likely to become so. Vagrancy, begging and cohorting with thieves and prostitutes was enough to get them locked away.

As the state took more of a role in education with the extensive building of secondary schools in the early 1900s, parents were increasingly expected to make sure that their offspring attended.

The First World War had a huge affect on communities, during and afterwards, as they struggled to come to terms with the huge loss of their men folk. During this time, schools continued to take more of a role in the physical and mental well-being of their pupils. Slowly, attitudes to the social and intellectual development of children became more sympathetic and less regimental, especially for the youngest.

By 1944 secondary education was provided for all free-of-charge with the leaving age set at 15. The 11-plus exam was introduced and the changes enabled working-class boys and girls to receive a secondary education with the chance of going on to university.

There were now formal provision for grammar, secondary modern and technical schools, such as the Bournville Boys' Technical School established in 1955. Nationally, few technical schools were in fact built.

Art of the matter *A young primary school pupil finishes off his picture created during an arts and crafts lesson on October 19, 1976*

Jump to it *Barry Clements taking part in the long jump event at the All Birmingham Deaf School Sports Day at Hadley Stadium, Smethwick, on May 24, 1972*

▲ **Write on** *A pupil at Elms Farm Infants School practices his handwriting skills on the blackboard in March 1964*

▲ **Petition campaign** *Wyndcliffe Junior School's lollipop man, Alfred Orme, puts his name to a petition organised by parents to save the job of a music teacher at the Bordesley Green school in June 1970*

Home time *Retiring headmistress Barbara Davies with some of the children at Allens Croft Nursery School in Kings Heath on July 14, 1980*

▲ **Spread the word** *Children at Ridpool Junior School in Kitts Green produced their own newspaper, The Bugle, as part of a media project in March 1985*

▶ **Chemical lessons** *A science lesson in progress at Waverley School in Small Heath, pictured in 1910*

▲ **On the ball** *Football-mad schoolgirls Faye Douglas, left, and Karen Rooney aged 10 and 11, who made their debut for their school Grendon Primary School in Kings Heath in the South Birmingham Junior Cup quarter-finals against Yardley Wood. They were picked to play for their school after impressing in practice matches against the boys. They are pictured on March 10, 1989*

▶ **Woodwork** *A teacher gives a little help to pupil John Crump, aged 14, during a woodwork lesson at a Birmingham school on March 2, 1971*

Cricket test *Schoolboys from Wyndcliffe Primary School in Bordesley Green attended England's test match against Australia at Edgbaston in June 1961*

Tucking in Saltley School pupils enjoying a healthy school dinner in June 1986

▲ **Great bake-off** Pupils of a Birmingham secondary school making biscuits during a home economics lesson on May 18, 1977

▲ **Story time** Pupils listen to their teacher reading on April 28, 1982

◄ **Net gains** Handsworth pupils warm up for the basketball skills section as part of the Lower School Superstar event on May 16, 1984

▲ **Exciting chapter** *Two girls enjoying their school reading books in August 1978*

Ordered lesson *A teacher keeps his eye on his pupils as they sit in the classroom drawing pictures on July 18, 1968*

Fun-loving city is a real party town

Brummies know how to enjoy themselves and, over the years, the city has enjoyed some truly memorable moments

Splashing time *Revellers celebrate the new year in Birmingham on January 1, 1973*

Brummies certainly know how to enjoy themselves, whether it's New Year celebrations in the city's squares or the many parades that take place.

Undoubtedly, the civic event of the year is the Lord's Mayor's Show. A family day which has for generations raised money for local charities while introducing the new mayor and bidding farewell to the outgoing dignitary.

Another big event is Birmingham Pride, which has grown from modest beginnings in 1999 to be one of the city's most flamboyant spectacles, attracting anything up to 100,000 party-goers and spectators and raising thousands for local charities as well as boosting the local economy.

Easily as raucous and good natured, and another huge crowd pleaser, is the city's world-famous St Patrick's Day Parade – a Celtic cultural feast of music and entertainment – which has grown over the years to be one of the biggest of its kind outside Dublin, attracting over 80,000 revellers a year.

Another "fun" event but, again, with serious intention is the city's Walkathon, which in 2013 was renamed Walk for Harry in recognition of 11-year-old Harry Moseley, of Sheldon, who died from a brain tumour but raised £500,000 for charity by making and selling bracelets.

The walk, organised by BRMB Radio (now Free Radio), regularly attracts 10,000 walkers.

But it would be wrong to think that the carnival spirit is something new in the city.

There has been a tradition of frivolity and high-jinx for generations. In fact, in the 19th century some of the city's boisterous antics were frowned upon and rather offended the sensibilities of the city's burgeoning middle classes. One such event was the Onion Fair.

Although, the origins of the fair began in the Bull Ring to coincide with the onion harvest – it was then called the Michaelmas Onion Fair – it eventually outgrew the city centre and its welcome with local businessmen who felt it was attracting trouble-makers and thieves. Under growing pressure it eventually settled at the Serpentine Grounds in Aston.

The fair was a boisterous, hullabaloo of waltzers, dodgems, side shows and the chance to entice an unsuspecting girl onto the ghost train! However, despite its name, it did not have much in the way of onions.

For many a Brummie it was the big event of the year and was excitedly anticipated by youngsters who would eagerly save up their pocket money for a go on the coconut shy.

One year there was extra excitement when a lion escaped from a side show. It seems there's nothing quite as heady as the smell of a fun fair with its mix of engine fumes, candyfloss and sizzling sausages.

In recent years, the anticipation of the touring funfair has given way to the convenience of the theme park. For many the earliest experiences of white-knuckle rides were gained at Drayton Manor in Staffordshire which opened in 1949.

Today, rides at the park are undoubtedly more hair-raising than those post-war with The Shockwave, which is Europe's only stand-up roller coaster, taking top bill.

Laughing policeman PC Chris McEvilly gets into the carnival spirit with Elaine Libard during the Handsworth Carnival on September 10, 1989

Centre of attraction Miss Birmingham at the Lord Mayor's Show in 1973

▲ *Colourful fun* Emelda Nelson from Bromford dances her way along the Handsworth Carnival procession on September 11, 1988

FLOATS WANTED

▲ *Carnival capers* Pupils of Fordbridge Infants School all set for Kingshurst Carnival aboard their float on May 24, 1988

▶ *Procession pride* The Lord Mayor's Show on Saturday, May 26, 1973

Evening Mail

The Birmingham Post

Sunday Mercury

▲ **Fancy dress**
From left, sisters
Pam Wilkins,
Lynn Phillips,
Lynn Knight and
Barbara Spencer,
from Ward End,
dressed up as
native Americans
at the 1987
Walkathon

▶ **Fair fun** A
view of the
Onion Fair at
the Serpentine
Grounds in Aston
on September 29,
1960

▲ **Loud and proud** *Dancers in Victoria Square during the city's Gay Pride parade in 2007*

◀ **Star attraction** *Boxing legend Muhammed Ali leading the way at the Walkathon in 1984*

▶ **Irish theme** *A scene from the St Patrick's Day Parade in March 1969*

Taken for a ride Margaret Rojo, centre, takes a ride on the carousel on the fairground at Cannon Hill Park during Birmingham's International Spring Festival on May 22, 1970

▲ **Hopes high** Revellers welcome in the new year in Chamberlain Place in 1967

◀ **High note fun** People join arms as they sing a chorus of Auld Lang Syne to welcome in the new year near the Hall of Memory in 1973

The way we were

Every Saturday in the Birmingham Mail, historian Carl Chinn looks back at how we used to live in decades past. Plus each day our amazing archive photographs tell the story of how we used to live and remind us of how the world looked. Never mind the rose-tinted spectacles, look back at 'the good old days' in the Birmingham Mail.

LOVE YOUR HISTORY?
LOVE BIRMINGHAM

Are you an expert on local history? Did you live through the Blitz? Do you know all about things like Birmingham's key role in the Industrial Revolution? If you have knowledge of any specific heritage subject, please get in touch and help play an important part in Britain's biggest-ever media heritage project. With your support, we will be bringing history back to life...

E-mail the Heritage Editor:

harri.aston@trinitymirror.com

Summer's day
Birmingham Botanical
Gardens, Edgbaston, in
July 1957

Play and relaxation at our great parks

Brummies have long sought refuge in our city's wonderful open spaces, whether it be for a gentle stroll, boating or some paddling pool fun

With the dirt and smog of industry it's no surprise city dwellers sought to escape the grime of their daily lives.

Opened in 1873, Cannon Hill Park was one such retreat. Originally meadowland, Louisa Ryland, daughter of a city industrialist, donated the fields to the citizens hoping that they would prove a source of healthful recreation to the people of Birmingham.

Two large lakes were constructed, along with smaller ornamental ponds and a bathing pool. More than 30 acres were devoted to ornamental gardens and shrub borders with Kew Gardens donating seeds and plants to establish a collection, to be studied by students of botany.

Of course, botany was already well established in Birmingham, with the Birmingham Botanical and Horticultural Society being founded in 1829 and the city's botanical gardens opening in 1832, with a zoological collection being added some years later.

An elegant glass Palm House was built in 1871, allowing palms and tree ferns to be housed and the gardens were soon a focal point of civic pride.

Whilst many city-dwellers must have wondered in awe at the strange and exotic at the botanical gardens, others sought the great outdoors by heading to Sutton Park.

Often described as Europe's largest urban park, its use over the centuries often mirrors the huge social changes nationally and shifts of political power locally. The recreational use of the park took off in the 1860s with the opening in 1862 of the Sutton Branch Line from New Street Station, allowing day-trippers easier access to the park, which quickly blossomed into an excursion favourite. The park would eventually get its own line and station and even a miniature railway.

At this time, there were boat and donkey rides, swimming, a funfair for the daring and formal gardens laid near Wyndley Gate for the more gentle pursuit of strolling. There were even two horse-race tracks and a nine-hole golf course provided on Meadow Platt.

During the two world wars, the park saw military use with thousands of troops, convalescents and even prisoners of war variously encamped on the site, sometimes in their thousands.

Thousands would again besiege the park in 1957 when, for two weeks, 32,000 noisy and very excited Scouts from 87 countries descended on Sutton Park for the World Jubilee Jamboree.

▲ Good old days
The paddling pool in Cannon Hill Park packed with toddlers while the mothers and aunties sit on the banks on August 2, 1955

Top man Len Salt, head gardener at the Birmingham Botanical Gardens, pictured on September 11, 1981

▲ **Horsing around** Horse riders splash through Powell's Pool, near the Boldmere entrance of Sutton Park, in 1962

◀ **Water fun** Family fishing from a boat on Bracebridge Pool, on the Four Oaks side of Sutton Park

▲ **Paddling away** Children playing on paddle boats in Sutton Park on July 29, 1962

▶ **Ride on** Children enjoying donkey rides in Sutton Park in July 1962

▲ **Up, up and away** An aerial view showing the start of the balloon race at Cannon Hill Park, an event which launched the city's first International Spring Festival on May 18, 1970

▶ **Fishing for fun** The first weekend of the coarse fishing season and sunny weather brings anglers out in force at Swanshurst Park, Kings Heath, on June 21, 1970

▲ *All action* A Royal Navy helicopter lifting out troops during a mock battle on the last day of the International Spring Festival at Cannon Hill Park on June 3, 1972

◄ *Wet and wild* Children playing in the swimming pool at Sutton Park in 1962

Pleasant scene A boat on the lake at Handsworth Park on a sunny day in March 1954

Summer joy A little girl splashes away with her mother in a stream just inside the main gate of Sutton Park in 1962

▲ **Relaxation** Two women sitting on a bench enjoying a conversation in Sparkhill Park in May 1952

◄ **Monument** The statue of Edward VII, originally in Victoria Square, now a prominent feature in Highgate Park in Balsall Heath in August 1953

▲ **Trunk business** *The park woodlands were only one of the many responsibilities of the foresters of Sutton Park*

Cooling off *Visitors enjoying the paddling pool in Small Heath Park on a hot summer day in July 1967*

From canals and rail to jumbo jets

Canals connected Birmingham to new markets and resources, while trams and trolleybuses were once a familiar sight trundling through the streets of the city

Atmospheric view *Rays of sunshine filter through the gaps in the roof at Snow Hill railway station in Birmingham in March 1967*

Today, it is difficult to imagine our canals were once the heartbeat of the industrial West Midlands. The city and surrounding region is indebted to the men who built the 160 miles of waterways and to the generations who worked them.

The latter were the boat people with deeply held traditions passed from father and mother to son and daughter. Diesel and steam replaced the tow horse in the early 20th century but for the preceding 150 years the horse had been an indispensable part of canal life.

Birmingham's rapid industrialisation and transformation to a metropolitan city is incredible considering that it neither had direct access to a sea port nor a navigable river. The canals connected Birmingham to new markets and resources.

Trains first ran between Birmingham and Liverpool in 1837; and between Birmingham and London in 1838. There soon followed the Birmingham and Derby Junction Railway and the Birmingham and Gloucester Railway.

Goods could reach new markets in half the time that it took by road and a fraction of that by canal. A journey from Birmingham to the capital by rail was less than five hours and manufactures seized upon the chance to seek out new markets. New Street Station was officially opened in 1854 and the original Snow Hill Station was also built in the 1850s. It served the Great Western Railway line but its importance diminished later and it closed in 1972 to be reopened in the mid-1980s.

Trams and trolleybuses were once a familiar sight trundling through the streets of Birmingham.

With one of the country's most extensive tram networks outside of London and with a fleet of more than 800 trams, the city and outlying areas were incredibly well served.

It was the largest narrow-gauge tramway network in the UK, boasting 20 depots. The first trams began operating in the city in the 1870s but by 1937 trams and trolleybuses were being phased out by motorbuses.

It was in 1928 that Birmingham City Council first proposed the idea of a municipal airport for the city. But it would be 11 years before the £250,000 airport at Elmdon would be officially opened. The airport was owned and operated by the city council with early services flying to Croydon, Glasgow, Liverpool, Southampton and Ryde and Shoreham.

By the 1970s the airport was dealing with a million passengers a year.

▲ Setting off
Miss ATV Pam Calver is pictured with members of the crew who were taking part in a weekend cruise around Birmingham in March 1973

▲ **Real adventure** Bordesley Green Cubs enjoying a day out on the Birmingham canals on April 10, 1954

▲ **City service** Birmingham's first steam tram, pictured in 1882

▶ **Easter getaway** Holidaymakers on the platform at Snow Hill Station awaiting the arrival of a train to Penzance, Cornwall in April 1954

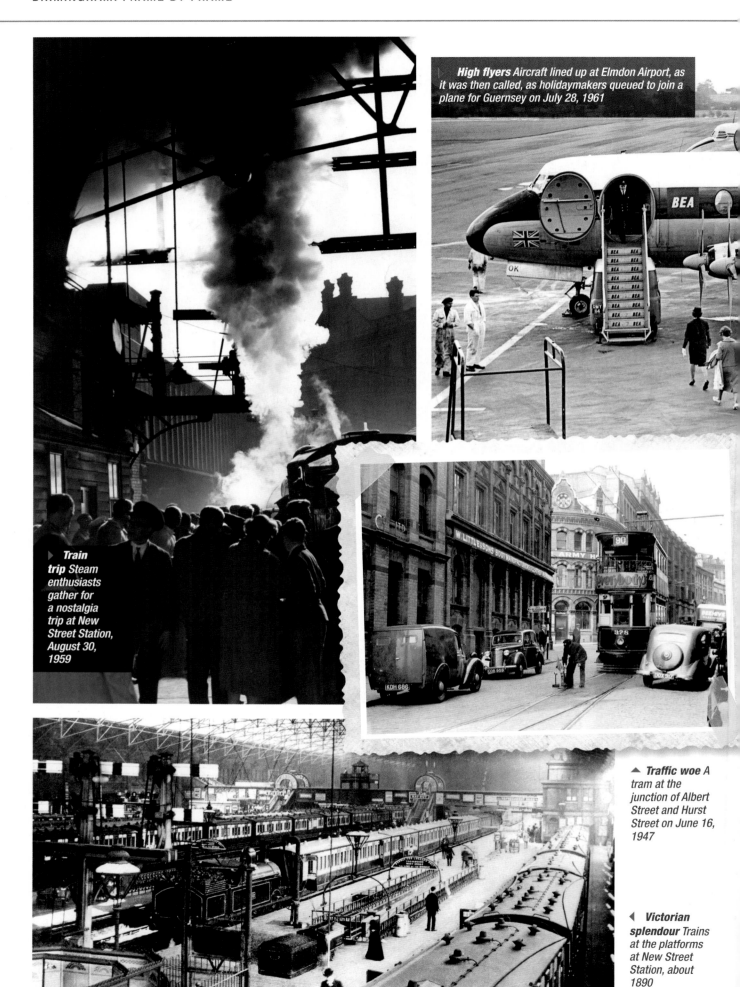

High flyers *Aircraft lined up at Elmdon Airport, as it was then called, as holidaymakers queued to join a plane for Guernsey on July 28, 1961*

▶ **Train trip** *Steam enthusiasts gather for a nostalgia trip at New Street Station, August 30, 1959*

▲ **Traffic woe** *A tram at the junction of Albert Street and Hurst Street on June 16, 1947*

◀ **Victorian splendour** *Trains at the platforms at New Street Station, about 1890*

▲ **Brew's up** *A female worker at Snow Hill serves a cup of tea from her refreshments trolley to a passenger at the window of his train carriage on May 31, 1949 – a service just introduced by the Western region of British Railways*

◀ **Romance of steam** *The LMS-built Jubilee 4-6-0 steam locomotive 45685 Barfleur departs from New Street Station on April 15, 1961*

▶ ***Maintaining order*** Lines of police on the streets in Digbeth, during confrontations between far-right political groups and ant-fascist campaigners in January 1978

The people who help keep us safe

It's difficult to think of life without our emergency workers but the fire, police and ambulance services are a relatively modern addition to life in Birmingham

What little boy hasn't stared wide-eyed as a fire engine races by with sirens wailing? Although today's machines have state of the art fire-fighting technology, it was often the 1960s Bedfords and Dennis's with their weighty red hulls that hugged the road, solid and reliable and perhaps a little heavy on the steering, which set the imagination buzzing.

It's difficult to think of a life without our emergency services; be they fire, ambulance or the police. But they are all comparatively modern, having evolved and grown as the city has grown and to meet ever-changing national policy.

For centuries, the risk of fire was an ever-present threat and fire-fighting was a haphazard affair with householders often left to rely on the goodwill of neighbours and friends. But as Birmingham grew and became industrialised, businesses and home-owners sought more reliable ways to protect their properties, and they turned to insurance companies to provide a fire-fighting service.

Increasingly, the City Corporation became involved in providing a public fire service and in 1875 the City of Birmingham Fire Brigade was founded. In 1941, Birmingham Fire Brigade merged with other fire brigades to form the National Fire Service.

In the early years, fire-fighting equipment was horse-drawn with water pumped manually. But by the 1850s the first steam-powered appliances started to appear. However, it wasn't until the turn of the 20th century that the first motorised vehicles would be seen on the streets of Birmingham.

Whilst early fire-fighting was initially left to market forces and volunteers, policing in the city did at least have deeply-enshrined Common Law to fall back on.

However, until 1839 the city did not have a regular police force. This was to change when an outbreak of Chartist rioting in 1839 so shook the city's establishment that magistrates called for back-up from the Metropolitan Police, which itself had only been operating 10 years.

Soon afterwards, the city was given powers to set up its own police force and appoint a chief commissioner empowered to recruit constables. The first police commissioner for Birmingham was appointed on September 1, 1839. He was local barrister Francis Burgess.

Men were quickly recruited as constables but the calibre of many was questionable and drunkenness was a major problem and accounted for a large number of dismissals.

The regime was highly militaristic with considerable time spent drilling and with unmarried recruits expected to live in barracks.

In 1974, following the reorganisation of the local authority boundaries, Birmingham City Police was incorporated into the newly-formed West Midlands Police.

▲ *Trusted figures* Beat policemen Roy Rippin, right, and Chris Such make friends with the children at Wychall Farm Infants School in Kings Norton after giving a demonstration in March 1982

▼ **Up to the job** *Four-footed PC Monty, jumping over the backs of PC Leslie Beckley and PC Cyril Roberts in January 1958*

▼ **Local bobby** *A policeman leaving his local police station on his bicycle in a photograph probably taken around 1914*

▲ **Let's dance** *Community police officer Jim Quinn was joined by female residents during the annual Ladywood Fun Day on July 12, 1985*

▲ **Blues and twos** *New police patrol cars with flashing blue lights in action are introduced on January 8, 1963*

▶ **'Ello 'ello** *Aspiring police officer Stephen Lane, 7, of Castle Bromwich, admires one of the police's XJ6 Jaguar cars with PC Paul Thacker in August 1982*

▲ **Horse power**
Firefighters aboard their horse-drawn steam fire engine, in a photograph taken around 1900

▶ **Modern machine**
Firefighters from Birmingham Fire Brigade with their engine at around the turn of the 20th century

▲ **Blazing horror** *Firefighters aim a high-powered jet at a blazing clothing factory in Birmingham city centre on March 7, 1984. More than 100 firemen tackled the blaze which destroyed a factory on Bromsgrove Street*

▶ **Brave duo**
Firemen Alan Rooney, left, and Clive James with the breathing apparatus they wore when they entered a blazing paint factory to remove bins of highly explosive nitrocellulose in July 1967

Service pride *Firemen with their engines at the Upper Priory headquarters in Birmingham in 1906*

◄ **Vital equipment** Ambulanceman Alan Butler shows a new life support unit to Councillor John Charlton, left, and James Ackers at the opening of the £250 000 Monyhull Ambulance Station in Kings Norton. Looking on is ambulanceman Andrew Rodgers on November 13, 1984

▼ **Crowd stopper** Lenny Henry, pictured with fellow comedian Don Maclean, right, and ambulance driver John Hudgell, is taken away on a stretcher during the official unveiling of the world's biggest ambulance outside the Grand Hotel in Birmingham

United workers Ambulance workers at the Henrietta Street depot in Birmingham in December 1978

▲ *Ready for action* Firefighters on board their vehicle in central Birmingham in January 1968

◄ *Name confusion* Residents in Erdington protested about their road with two names, causing problems and delays for ambulance drivers. The road on the Wyrley Birch Estate had one side signposted Millbank Grove and the other side Faulkners Farm Drive. This picture was snapped on December 5, 1974

The Brum bands who conquered the world

The history of rock music has been littered with talented performers and musicians who have helped shaped the soundtrack of our times

New Romantics Duran Duran fans watch the band in concert at Villa Park in July 1983

▲ **Reggae icons**
*Birmingham's
UB40 in the
recording studio
in 1985*

New Romantics Duran Duran were at the height of their pop career when, on July 23, 1983, they staged an open-air benefit concert at Villa Park in front of 18,000 adoring fans.

Roger Taylor, Nick Rhodes and John Taylor all grew up in the city and the band had launched their meteoric rise from the Rum Runner club in Broad Street, which was at the centre of Birmingham's New Romantic sub-culture.

Duran Duran were undoubtedly the golden boys of the 1980s but by then Birmingham's music scene was already well established and easily rivalled that of London, Manchester and Liverpool.

There had been a steady stream of influential bands and singer song-writers emerging from the city since the Brum Beat era of the 60s when the Moody Blues career launched from the now legendary music venue Mothers, which was inauspiciously located above a furniture store in Erdington High Street.

Mothers was acclaimed as one of the most significant progressive rock clubs outside of London and is where Aston's Ozzy Osbourne and Tony Iommi's pioneering heavy metal band Black Sabbath played some early sessions.

During this time another powerhouse of music was evolving. Shard End-born Jeff Lynn and Roy Wood, from Kitts Green, would take the Move and then the Electric Light Orchestra in a completely different direction musically with the help of drummer Bev Bevan. Wood would also later go on to form glam rock band Wizzard.

With the demise of Mothers in the early 70s, Barbarella's in Cumberland Street would become the place to be seen and heard.

Birmingham was already a hard rock stronghold but the punk era was in full flow and any band worth its weight in black leather or safety pins played the venue including Blondie, AC/DC, The Stranglers The Sex Pistols, The Clash, Siouxsie and the Banshee's, The Ramones, The Buzzcocks and local punks The Killjoys, forerunner of Dexys Midnight Runners.

The club was immortalised when in 1978 Dire Straits recorded their first live album called Birmingham at Barbarella's.

Although by the 70s, punk was in full thrash, it wasn't the only music being heard on the streets and clubs.

Reggae had a strong place in the hearts of multi-cultural Birmingham and by the summer of 1978 a group of friends linked to the Moseley School of Art began rehearsing. Ali Campbell, Earl Falconer, Brian Travers and James Brown were among a small group of youngsters who would be joined by Ali's brother Robin to form UB40.

UB40 were unashamedly political and outspoken and so began another unique and successful chapter in the city's music scene.

▲ **Big stars** Duran Duran pose for the Mirror Rock and Pop Awards in February 1983

◄ **Young stars** Musical Youth, who took the charts by storm in the early 1980s with their distinctive reggae sound

◄ **Feel the noise** Black Country rock group Slade during a visit to Birmingham in March 1977. From left, Noddy Holder, Jimmy Lea, Dave Hill and Don Powell

▲ **Rock royalty**
Heavy metal group Black Sabbath with the silver discs they received for the album Technical Ecstasy. Tony Iommi, Ozzy Osbourne, Geezer Butler and Bill Ward pictured on August 10, 1977

▶ **Steel Pulse**
From left, Steve Nisbett, Basil Gabbidon, Michael Reilly, Selwyn Brown, Dave Hinds, Phonso Martin and Ronnie McQueen of Steel Pulse, pictured in Handsworth, where they are all from, on February 22, 1978

▲ **Blues stars** Steve Winwood celebrated his 18th birthday with his Spencer Davis Group bandmates by drinking a yard of ale. Pictured, from left, are Peter York, Spencer Davis and Muff Winwood on May 13, 1966

▶ **Prince of darkness** Ozzy Osbourne performing on stage during a concert in August 1981

◀ **Out of this world** The Tornados, from left, Heinz Burt, George Bellamy, Birmingham-born Roger LaVern, Alan Caddy and Clem Cattini with fans looking in through the window of the foyer at the Alpha Television Studios, Aston, on December 10, 1962

▶ *Moving on* Birmingham's Electric Light Orchestra fronted by Jeff Lynne, after Roy Wood's departure, and with Bev Bevan on drums. Pictured here at the NEC on March 15, 1986

▲ *Dazed and confused*
Led Zeppelin singer Robert Plant performing on stage during a concert at the Royal Albert Hall in London in June 1969

▲ *Thumbs up*
The Moody Blues in January 1964. From left, Michael Pinder, Clint Warwick, Denny Laine, Ray Thomas and Graeme Edge.

◀ *Moseley band*
Ocean Colour Scene play at the Hard Rock Cafe on Broad Street in April 2007 From left, Steve Cradock, Simon Fowler, Dan Sealey and Andy Bennett

▲ **Come on Eileen** *Dexys Midnight Runners, including Pete Williams (bass), Bobby Ward (drums), Pete Saunders (piano/organ), Geoff Blythe (tenor saxophone), Steve Spooner (alto saxophone), Jim Paterson (trombone) and Kevin Rowland (vocals), pictured in 1980*

◄ **Jumping for joy** *After The Move and ELO, Roy Wood, from Kitts Green, fronted his new band Wizzard, seen here on January 22, 1973*

▶ *Goods for sale* Busy scenes at the Bull Ring market in a photograph believes to have been taken in the 1920s

Looking back on how we shopped

Stores have come and gone but, with the huge Bullring centre at its heart, Birmingham remains one of the country's top shopping destinations

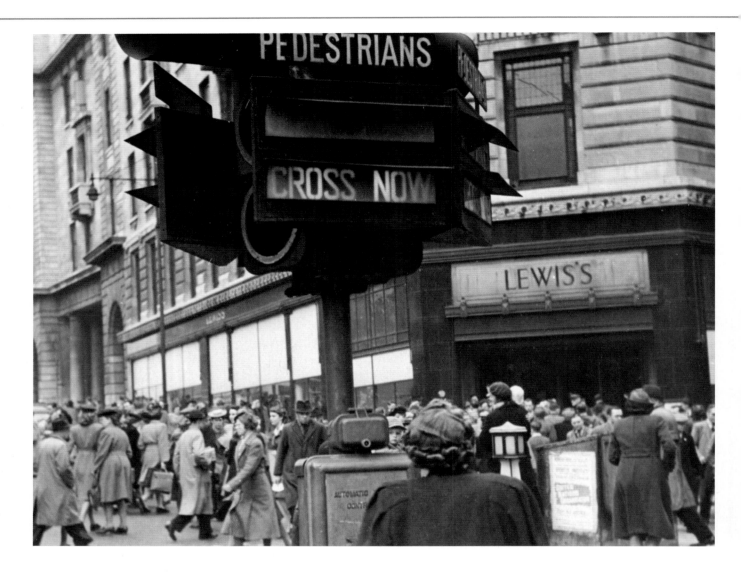

For the city's children, the magic of Christmas was made all the more remarkable with a trip to see Santa Claus at his fairyland grotto in Lewis's department store on the corner of Bull Street and Corporation Street.

Lewis's was a place where memories were made; of afternoon tea with aunty and a short back and sides at the hair salon. The store had everything and was a grand place to browse and spend a happy afternoon inspecting the latest Meccano sets on display in the toy department. There were even real animals on special occasions.

The store was originally opened in 1885, apparently at the behest of Liberal politician Joseph Chamberlain who was keen to invigorate that part of the city centre. Over the decades, Lewis's was refurbished and rebuilt several times and was considered the pinnacle of refined shopping. Sadly, it closed in 1991.

Rackhams, now House of Fraser, was another department store with its roots firmly set in Victorian Birmingham. From humble beginnings as a drapery shop at 78 Bull Street in 1851, it grew into a flourishing and extensive business. Badly damaged by a direct hit during the Second World War, it was sold to Harrods Ltd in 1955 which was itself taken over by House of Fraser. By the late 1960s an enlarged store was attracting record numbers and is still a favourite with shoppers.

As well as the big department stores, there were many smaller businesses which were equally important to the city economy. Wimbush's bakery in Small Heath, with its associated shops, are still a vivid recollection for many as are the Withers tobacconist shops which still have a presence in the city centre at the Great Western Arcade.

Wrensons the greengrocer – "the store where your money buys more" – was another familiar sight in the city from 1909 right into the 1970s. In the early days there was fresh ground coffee, sugar sold by weight in blue bags and delivery boys in white aprons cycling heavily-laden carrier bikes. And of course it sold Lux toilet soap!

Another well-respected greengrocer of the time was George J Mason, who opened his first shop in Lozells Road and went on to have stores scattered across Birmingham and further afield. The window displays of hung meats and groceries were truly from another era. Perhaps some people will recall his well-stocked delivery vans.

Stores have come and gone but arguably the biggest shock was the closure of Woolworths in 2009. Woolworths had a special place in the hearts of Brummies. The company had opened its flagship store in 1921 in Spiceal Street – a street which was itself steeped in history. It was immediately a big hit, generating some of highest sales in the country. Woolworths went on to become a major player in the development of the Bull Ring Centre in the 1960s.

▲ **Store that had everything**
Busy crowds outside Lewis's store, at the corner of Bull Street and Corporation Street, April 1946

▶ **Reeling in customers**
Fishmonger Albert Pearce serving his customers at Birmingham's new retail market on November 16, 1963

Bag them up *Italian women bagging onions at the wholesale market in Moat Row on June 1, 1901*

Heaving Busy scenes as shoppers cross the Corporation Street, Bull Street junction in 1955

▲ **So much choice** A woman looking at a packets of tea bags at a Birmingham supermarket in around 1965

◄ **Hunting for a bargain** The big rush for the beginning of the New Year sales in Lewis's store on December 30, 1971

As it was Shoppers in the Bull Ring area in 1930

Queuing up A long line of customers queue up outside the Rackhams store as the New Year sales begin in January 1973

▶ **Quiet period** *Normally bustling with Christmas shoppers, the Bull Ring area struggled to pull in the crowds on December 13, 1957*

▼ **Bread delivery** *A deliveryman for Harding's bakery is pictured in Byron Road, Small Heath, in around 1920*

▲ **Shopping street** A general view of Corporation Street, showing some of the shops including C&A, ABC Warehouse and H. Samuel jewellers on July 22, 1983

▼ **Walk this way** A spiral walkway was the modern method of getting to the new array of shops at the redeveloped Bull Ring Centre in the 1960s

▲ **Super shops** Shoppers at Birmingham's Pavilion Centre in November 1987

PURCHASE ANY PHOTO FROM THIS MAGAZINE

PERFECT GIFT FOR YOUR LOVED ONE

PHOTO··········
7
9
10
AVAIL
£9.5
+

············· PHOTO SALES ·············

If you would like to purchase a print featured wit
this publication contact our photosales team o